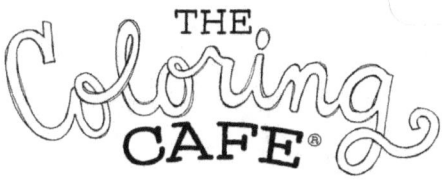

THE Coloring CAFE®

Cuties

Paper Dolls to
Color and Cut

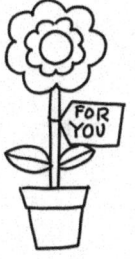

The Coloring Cafe-Paper Dolls/Everyday Fun/Ronnie Walter
ISBN: 978-0-9968291-8-2

A note from Ronnie

Hello!

Welcome to the fun of Paper Dolls! Wendy, Whitney, Willow and Wyn are four friends who love to share outfits—and go on adventures!

Use your imagination and design the outfits you'd want to wear--and remember all the outfits fit all of the girls—and you get to decide who wears what depending on their (and your) personality!

I hope you enjoy coloring and playing with these four friends as much as I did drawing them for you!

Happy Coloring,

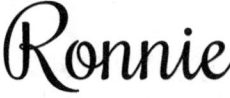 

www.thecoloringcafe.com

A few tips from Ronnie...

1) I like to color the pages while they are still in the book. Once you have colored the page, you should cut the whole page out of the book on the dotted line, and then cut out each individual piece. Don't forget to leave the tabs on the clothes because that's how they will stay on your doll.

2) If you prefer, you can start by cutting pages out of the book first and then coloring them, this works great for a group coloring together. When finished, cut out each individual piece (being careful to leave the tabs on the outfit).

3) If you are using markers, be sure to slip a separate piece of paper between the pages. The marker might bleed through the paper which could ruin the next page!

4) Colored pencils, fine tipped markers and gel pens are probably the best supplies to use. You can use crayons if you like, but they can be difficult to fit into the smaller spaces.

5) But really, however you want to do it is fine, so have fun!

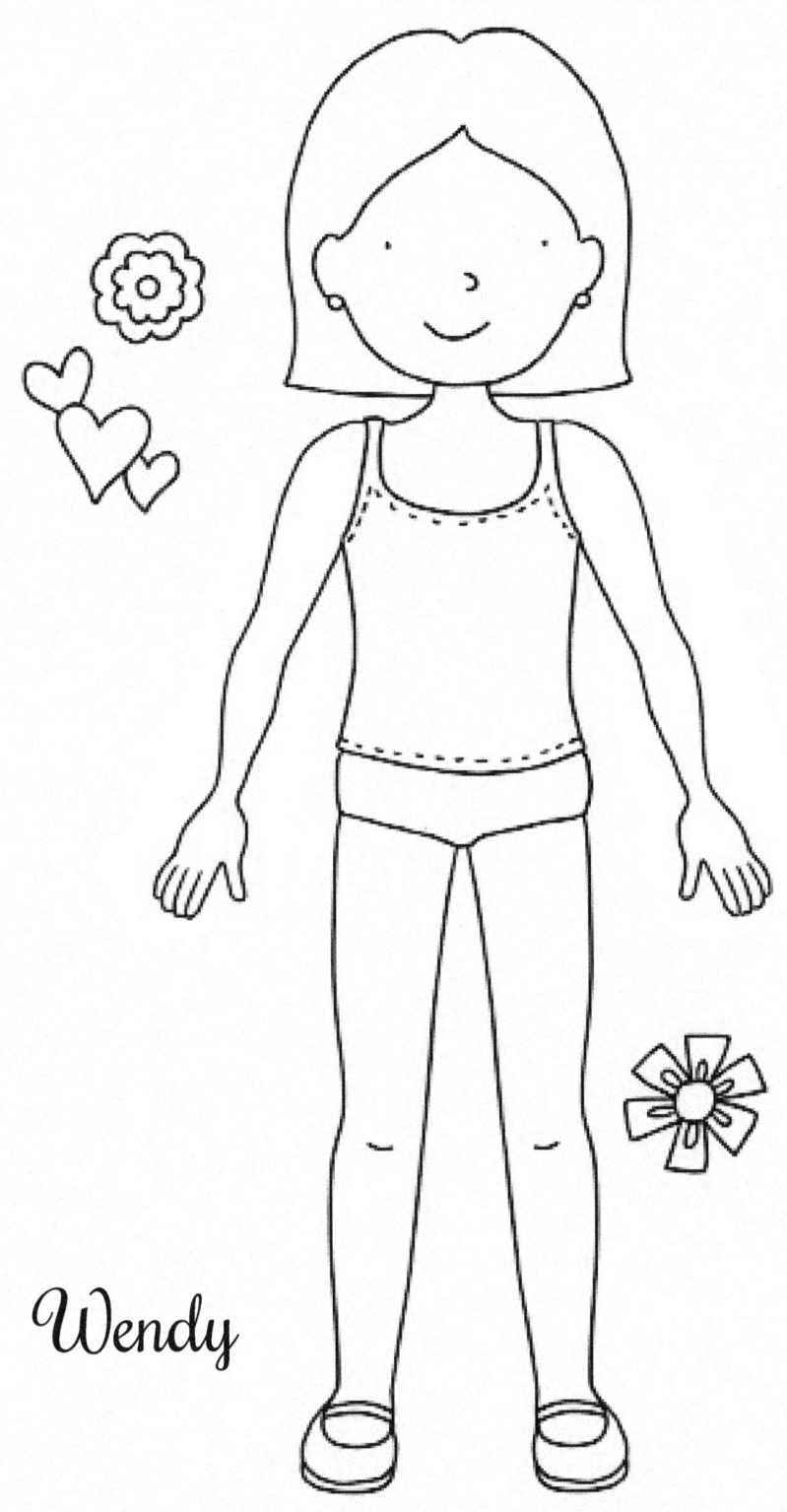

Wendy

The Coloring Cafe Cuties-Everyday Fun!

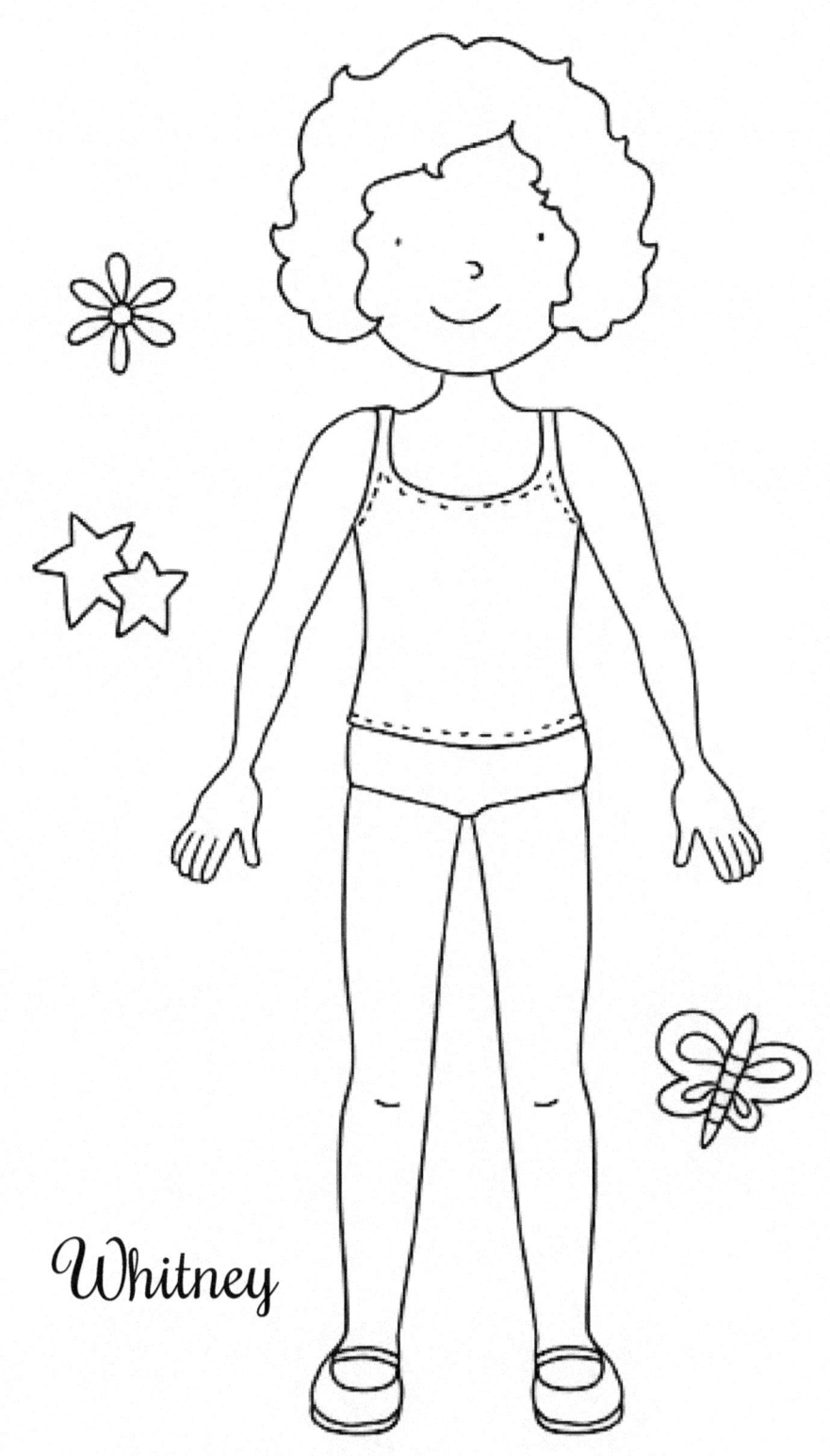

Whitney

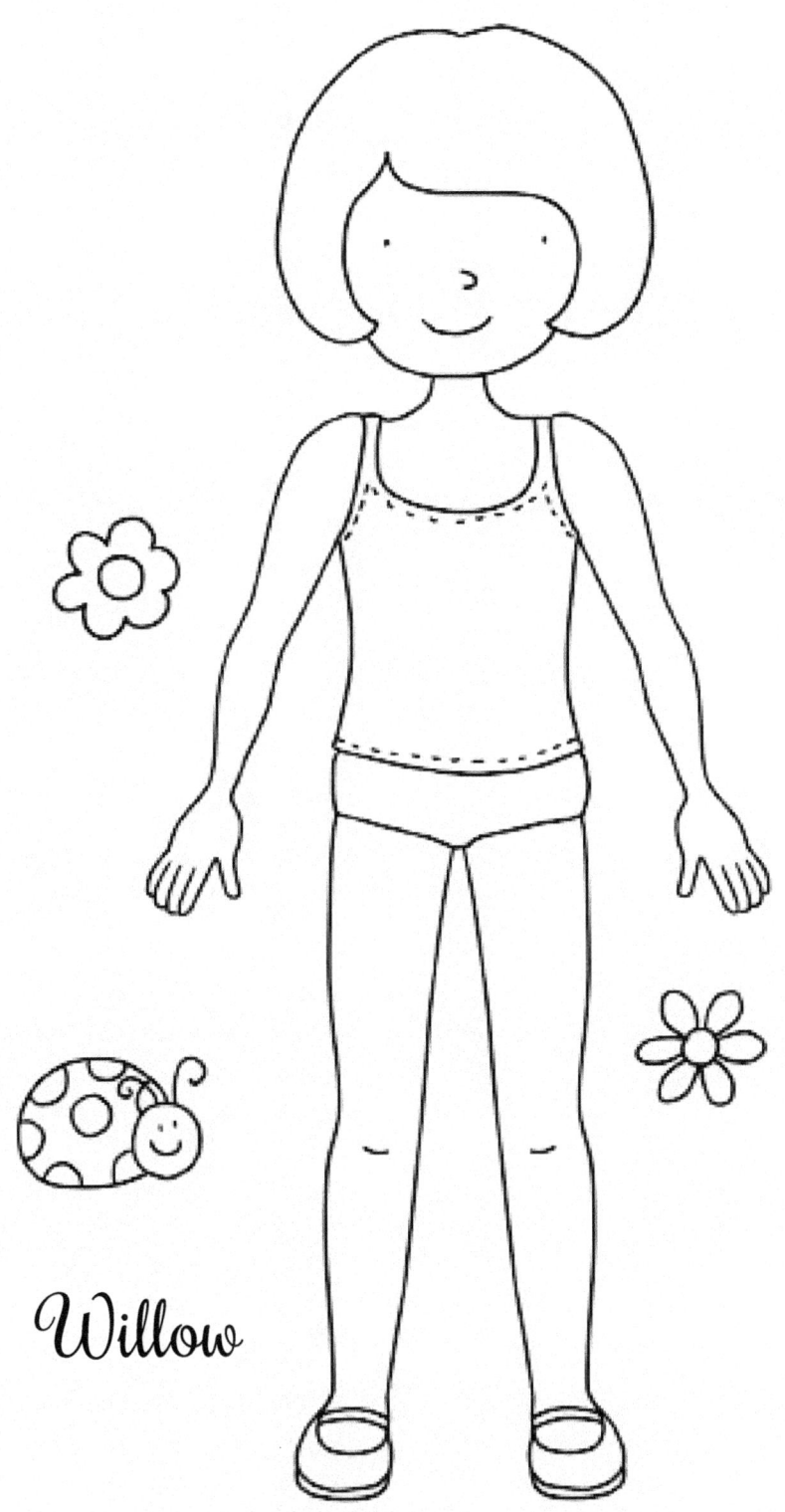

Willow

The Coloring Cafe Cuties-Everyday Fun!

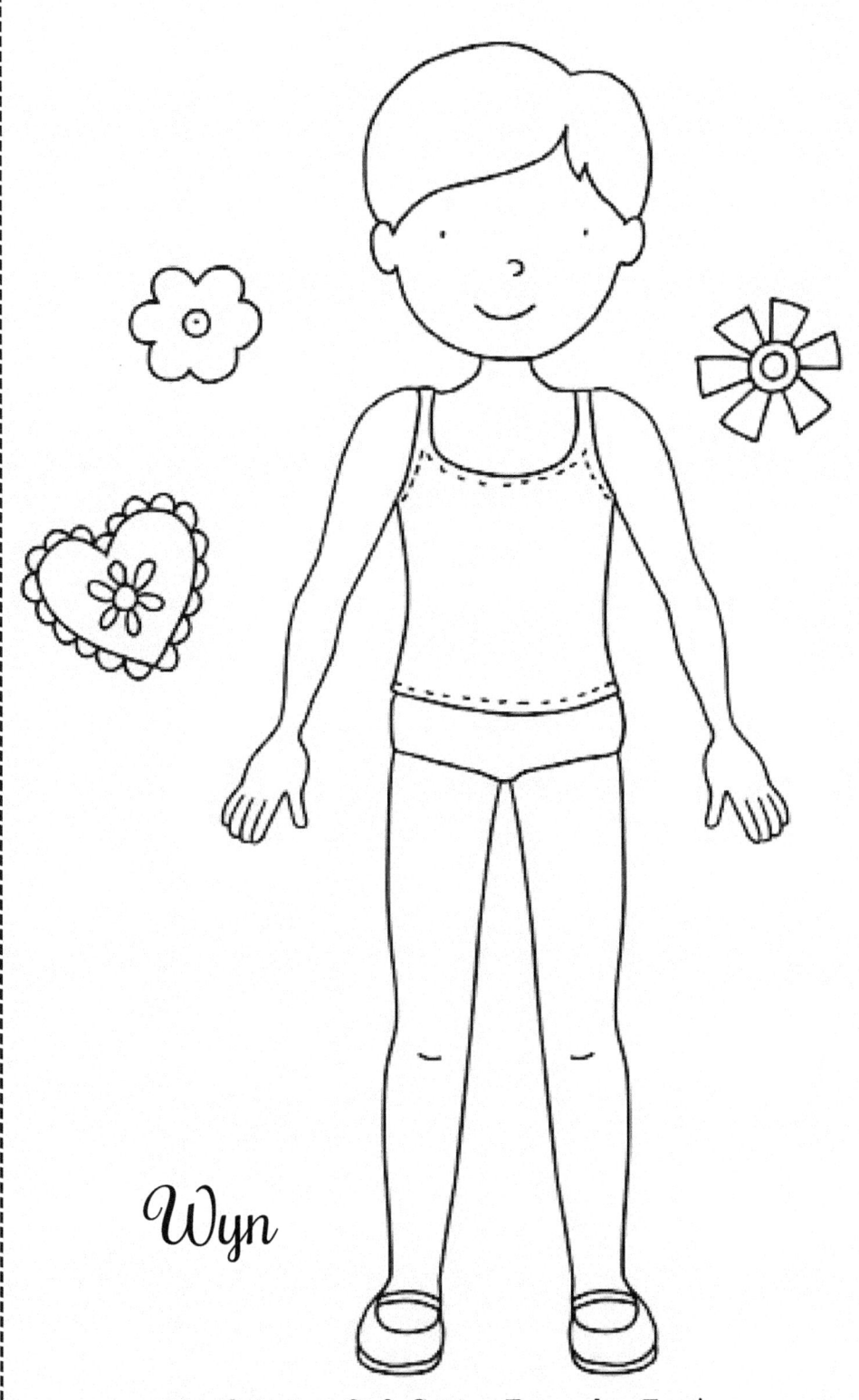

Wyn

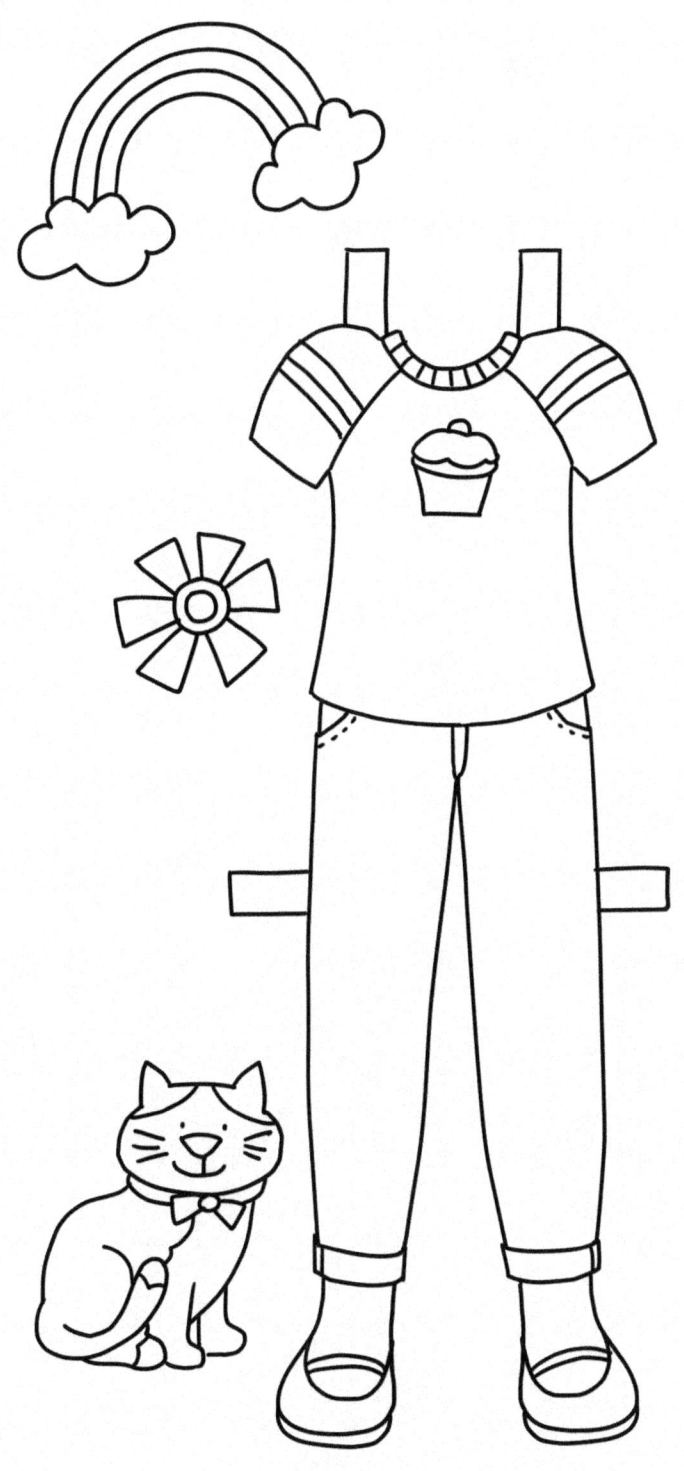

The Coloring Cafe Cuties-Everyday Fun!

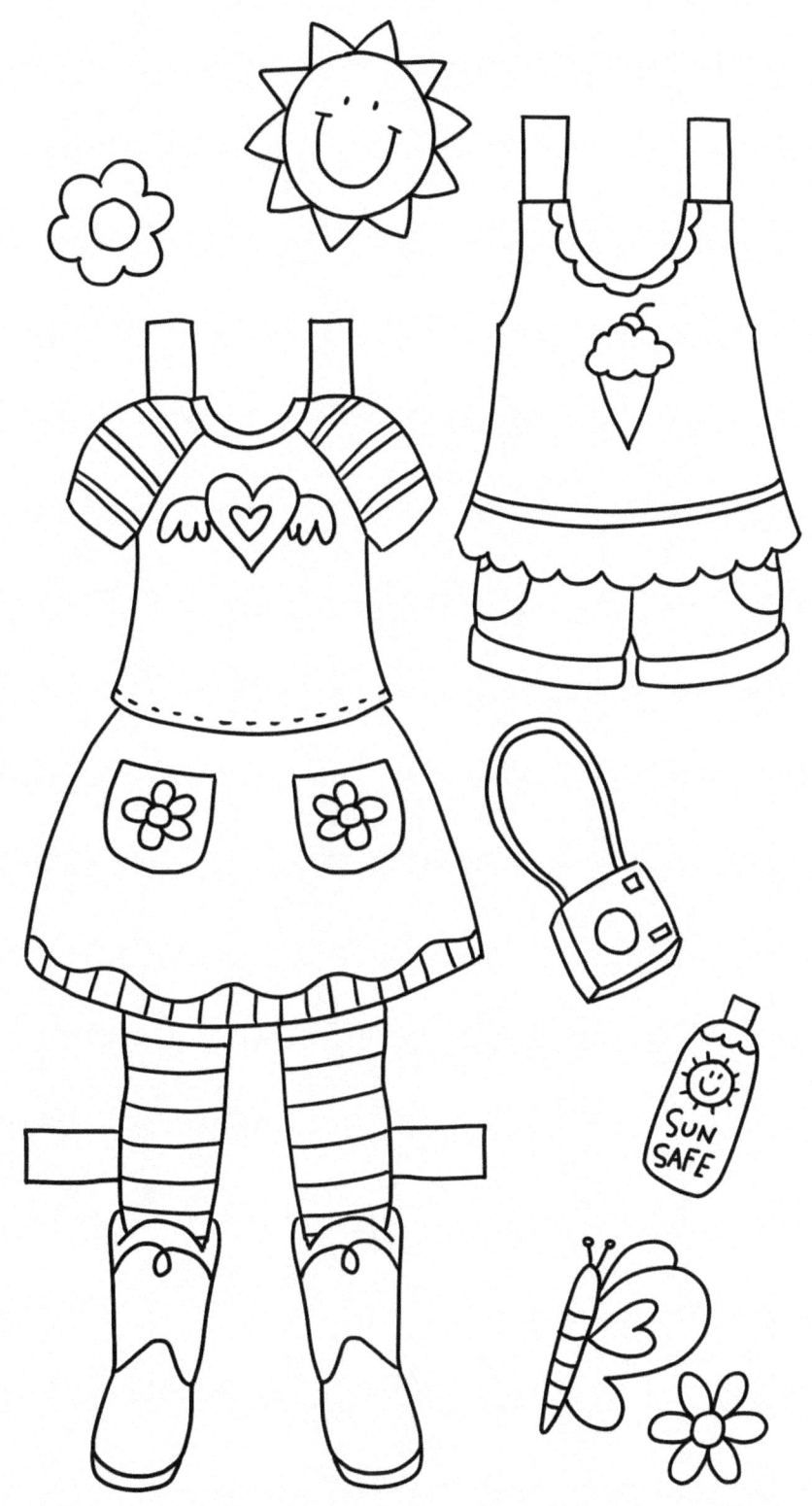

The Coloring Cafe Cuties-Everyday Fun!

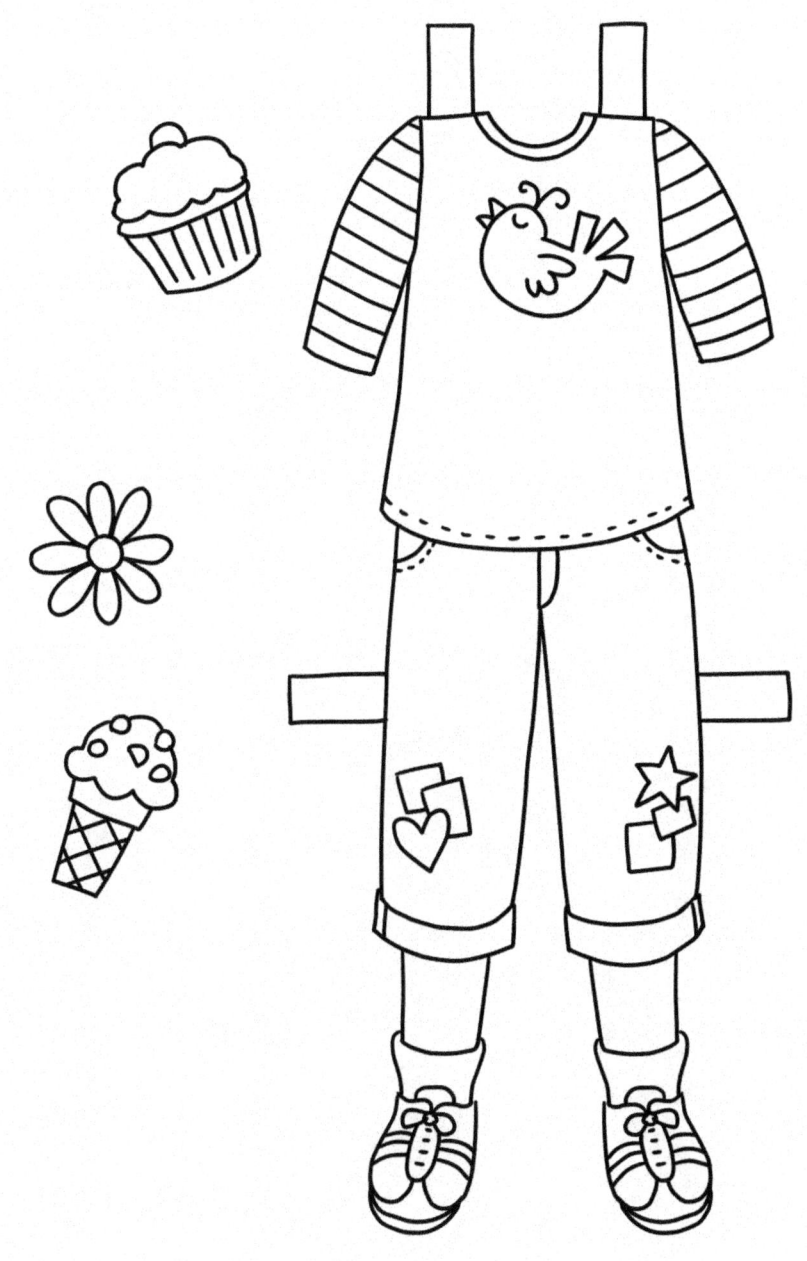

The Coloring Cafe Cuties-Everyday Fun!

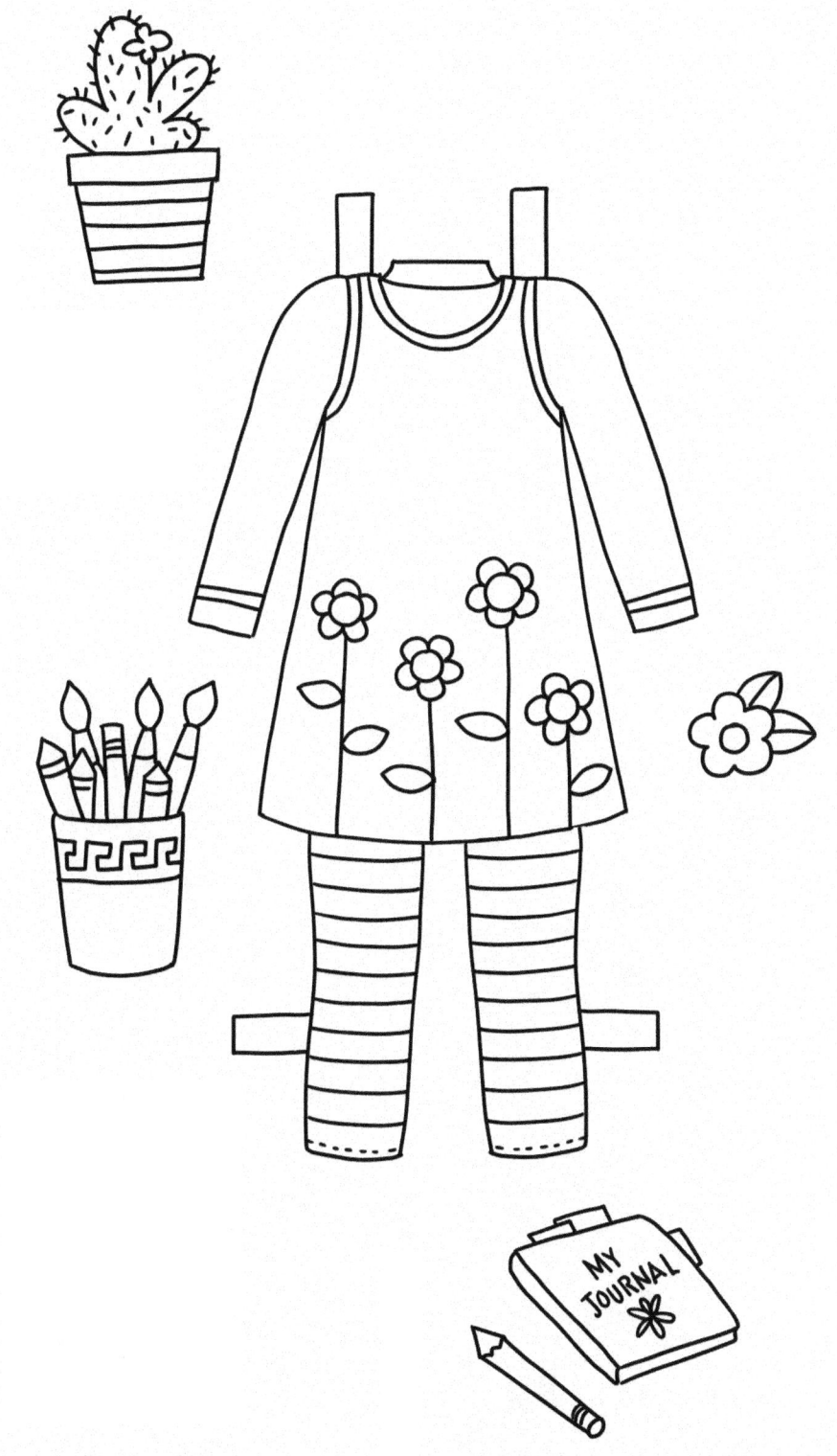

The Coloring Cafe Cuties-Everyday Fun!

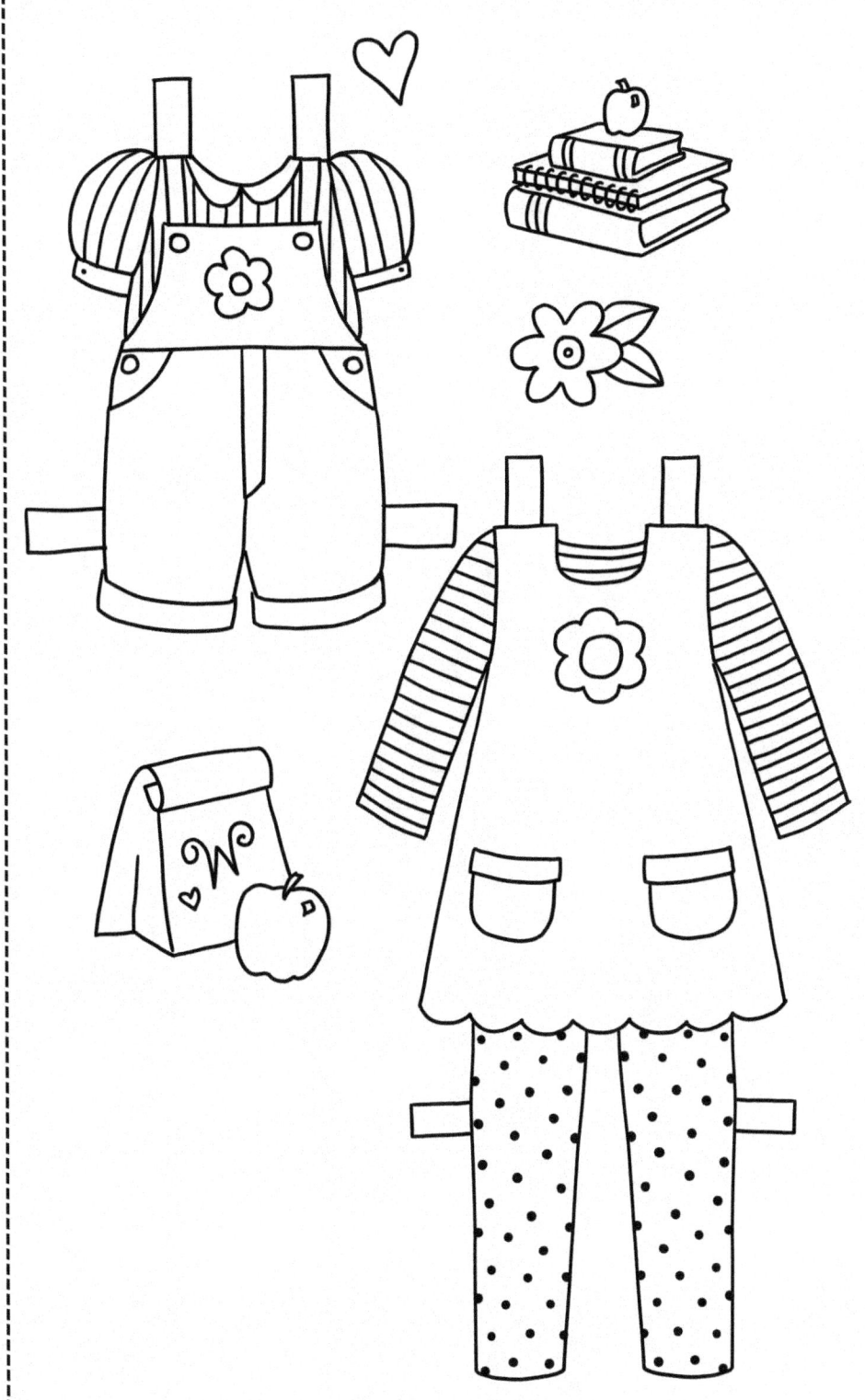

The Coloring Cafe Cuties-Everyday Fun!

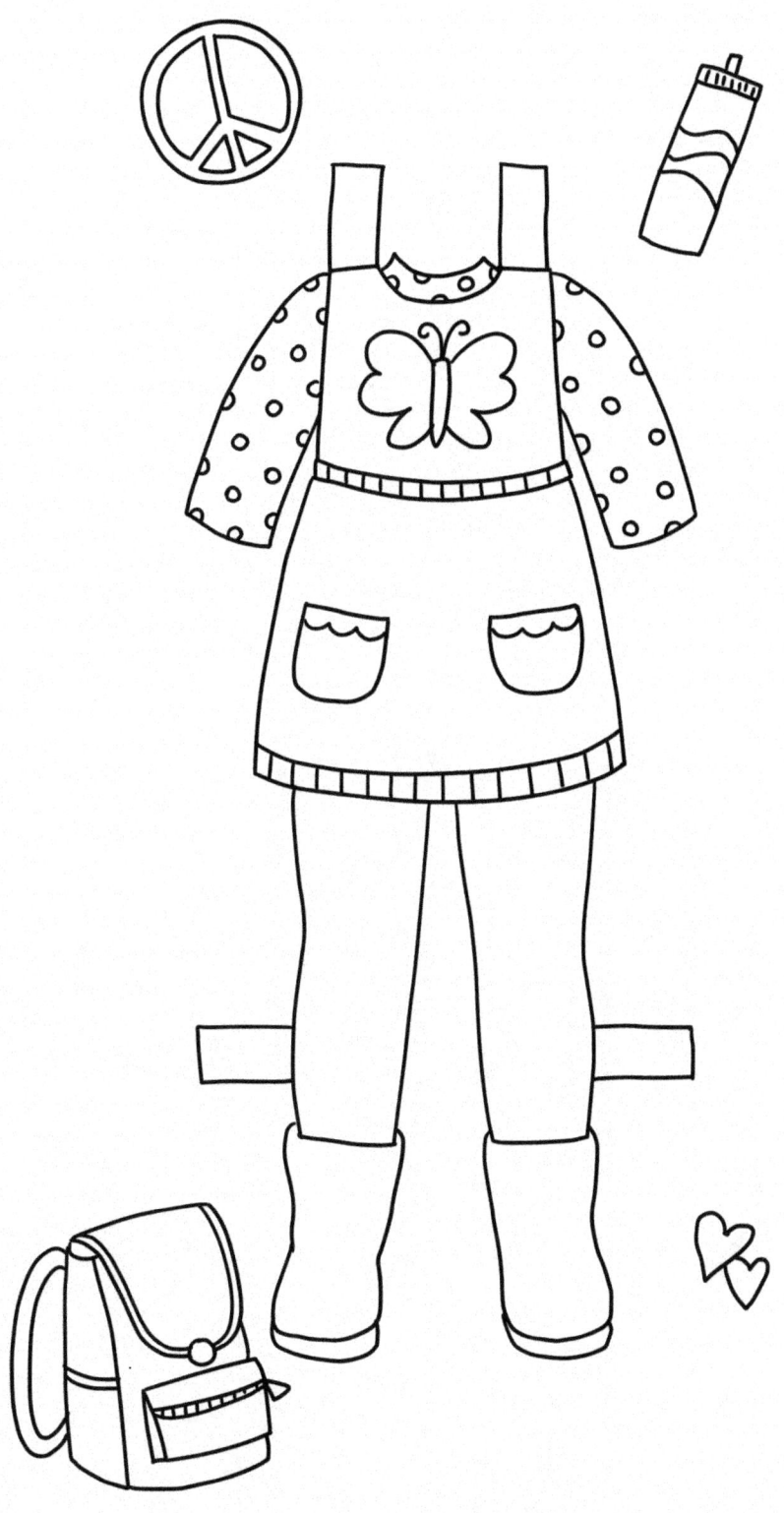

The Coloring Cafe Cuties-Everyday Fun!

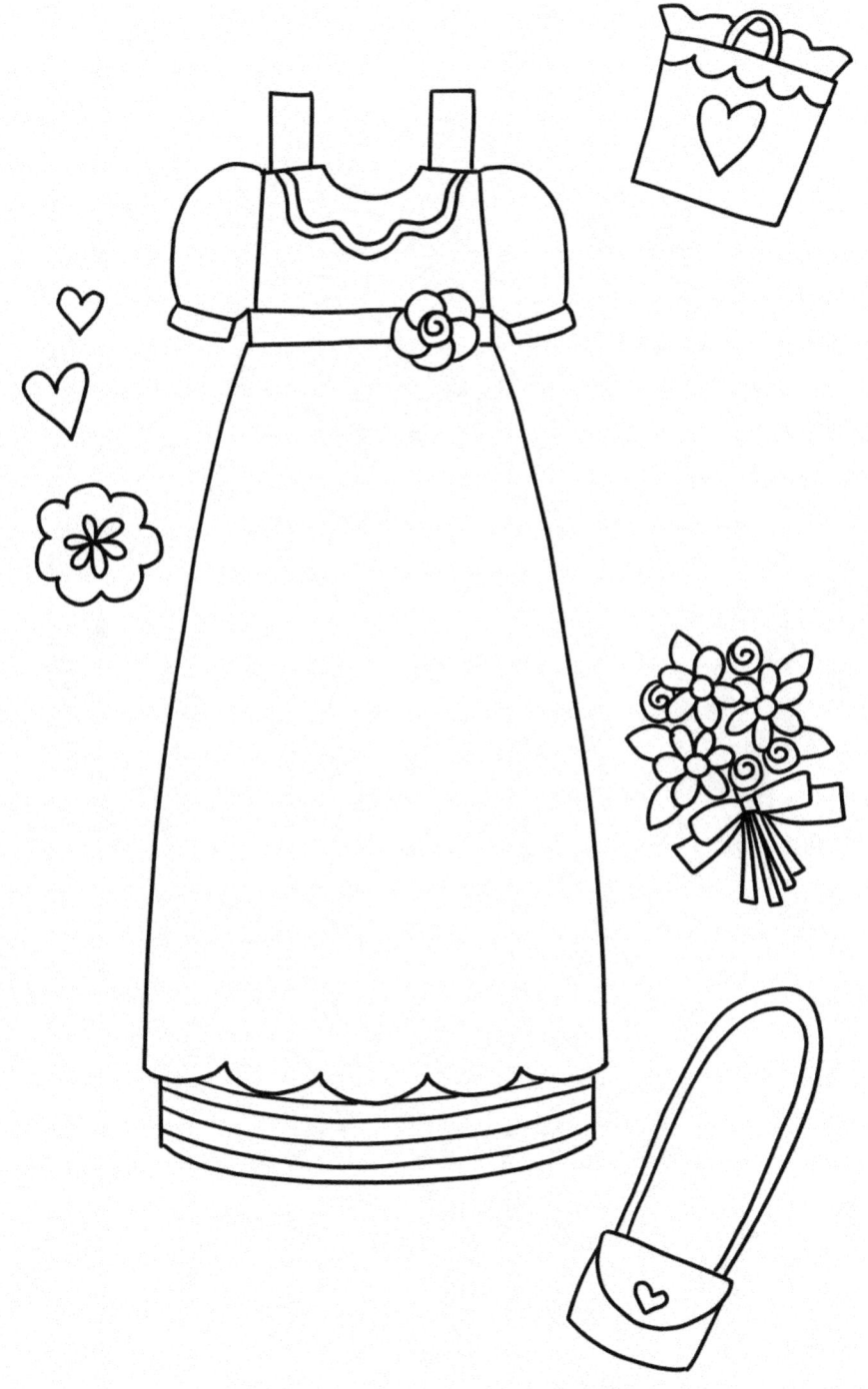

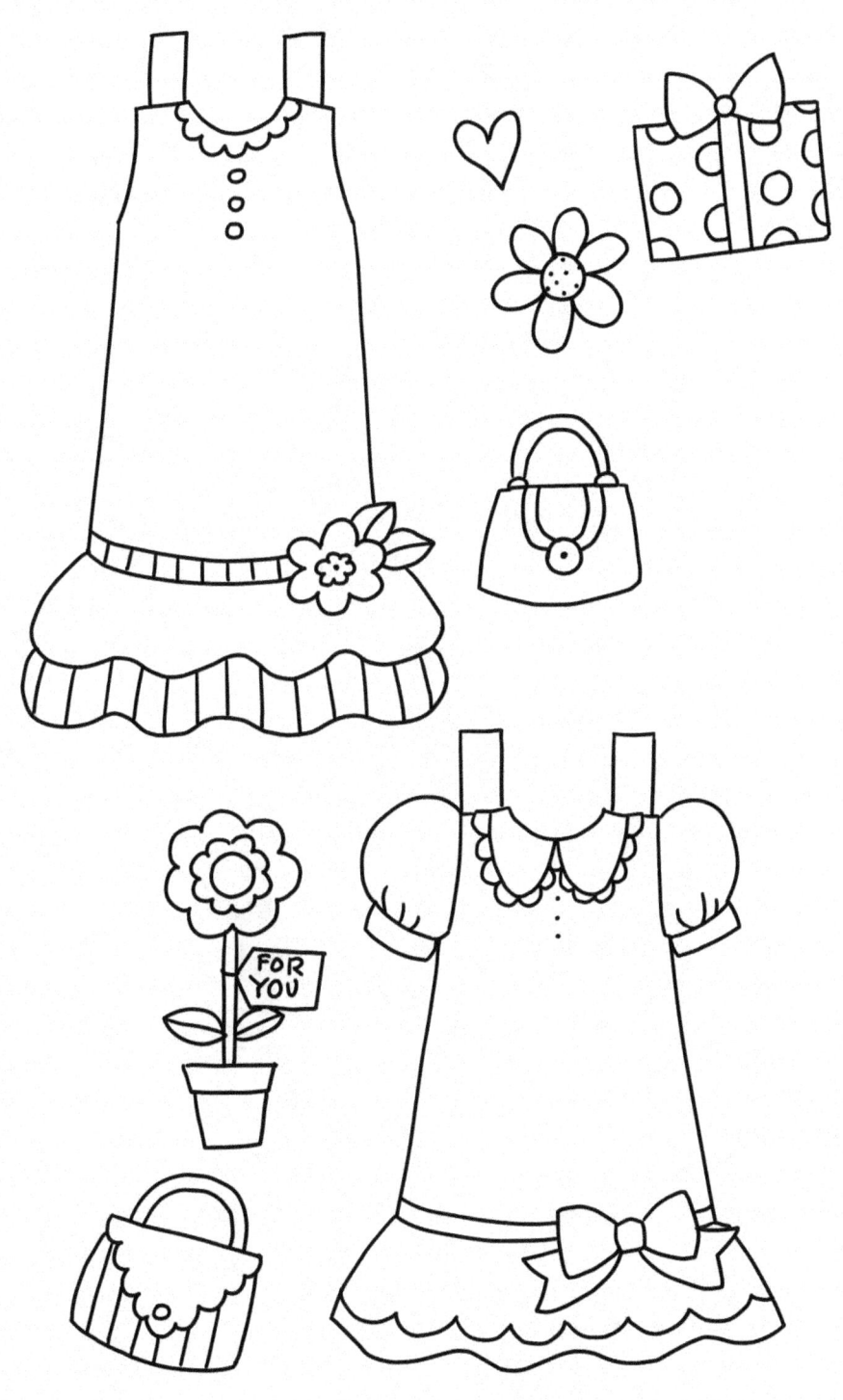

The Coloring Cafe Cuties-Everyday Fun!

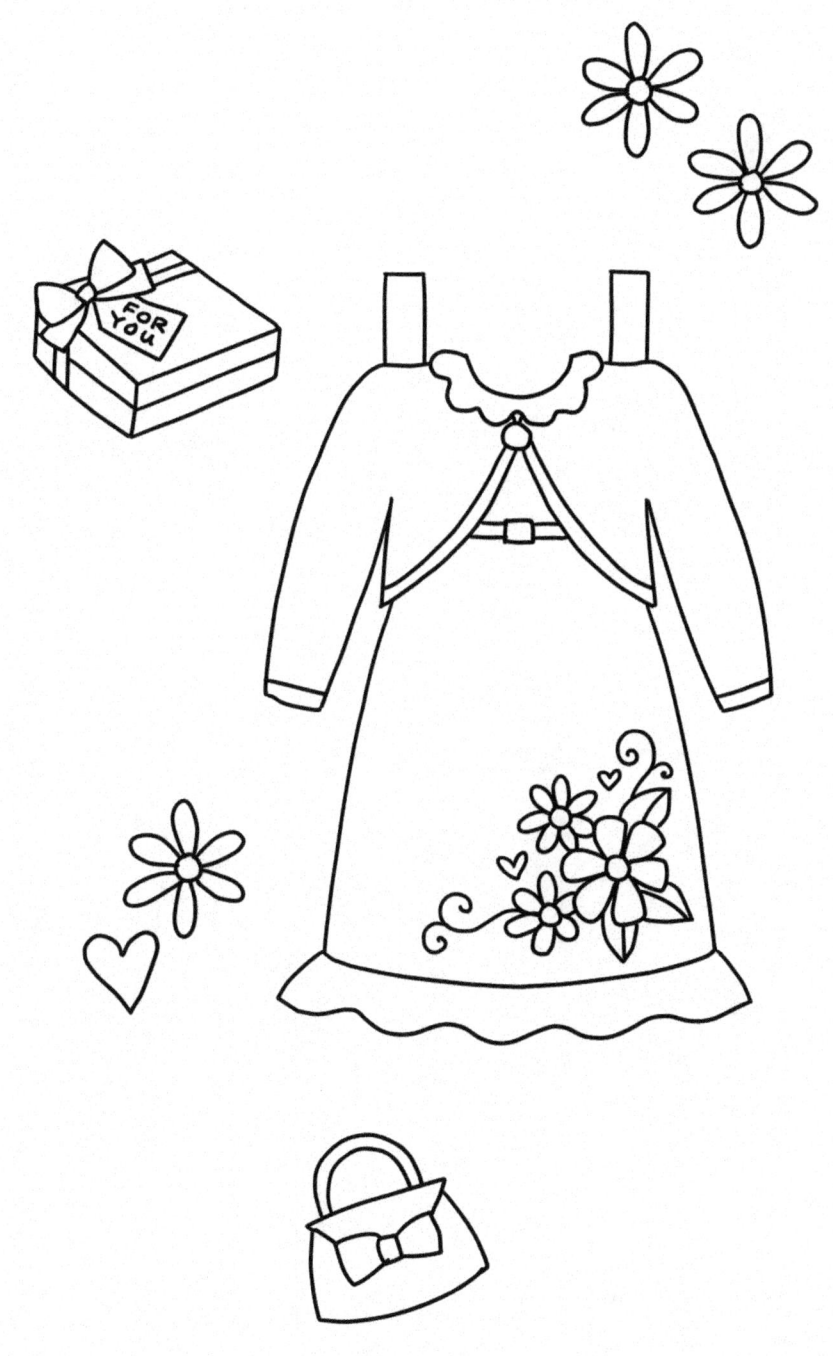

The Coloring Cafe Cuties-Everyday Fun!

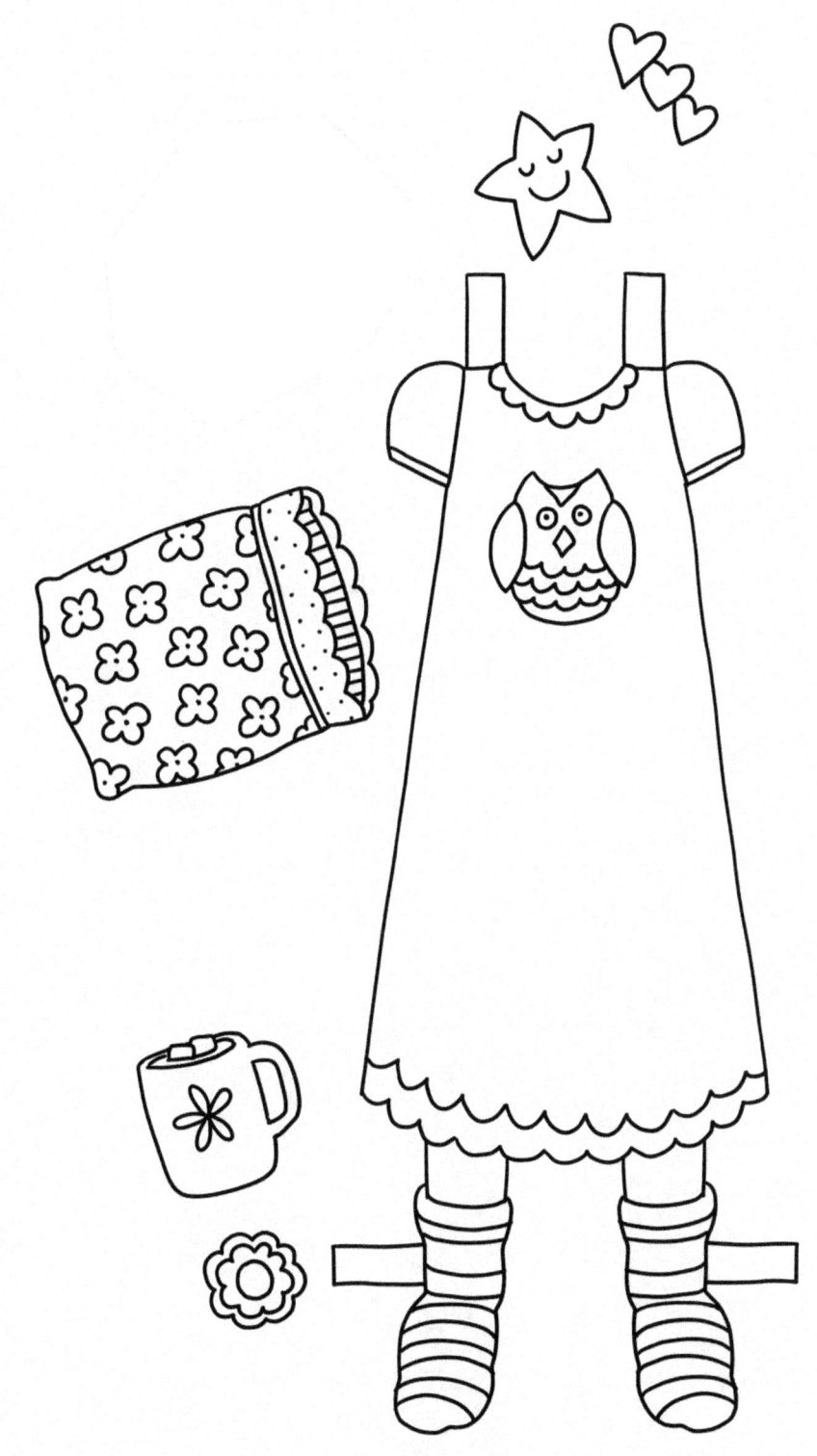

The Coloring Cafe Cuties-Everyday Fun!

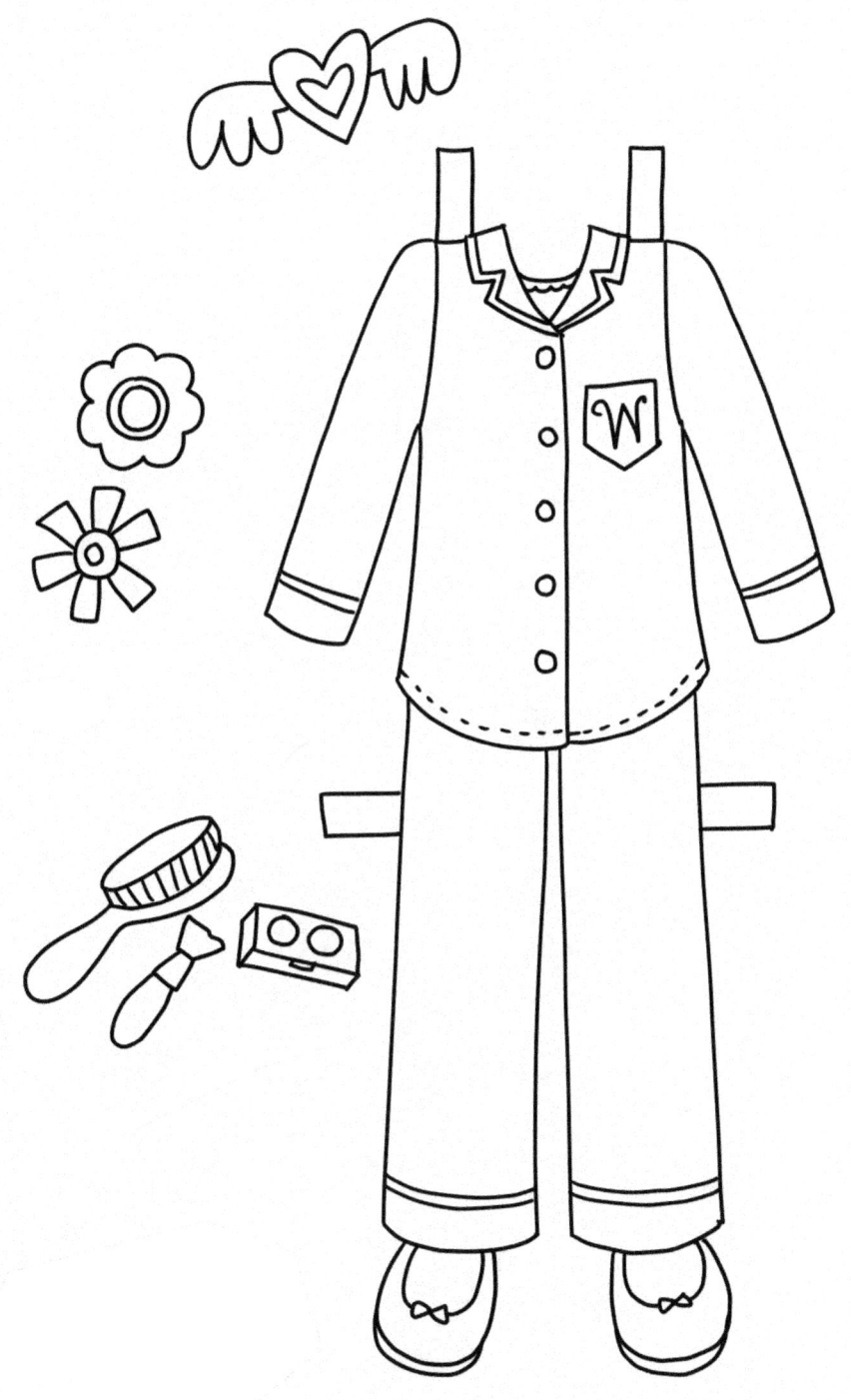

The Coloring Cafe Cuties-Everyday Fun!

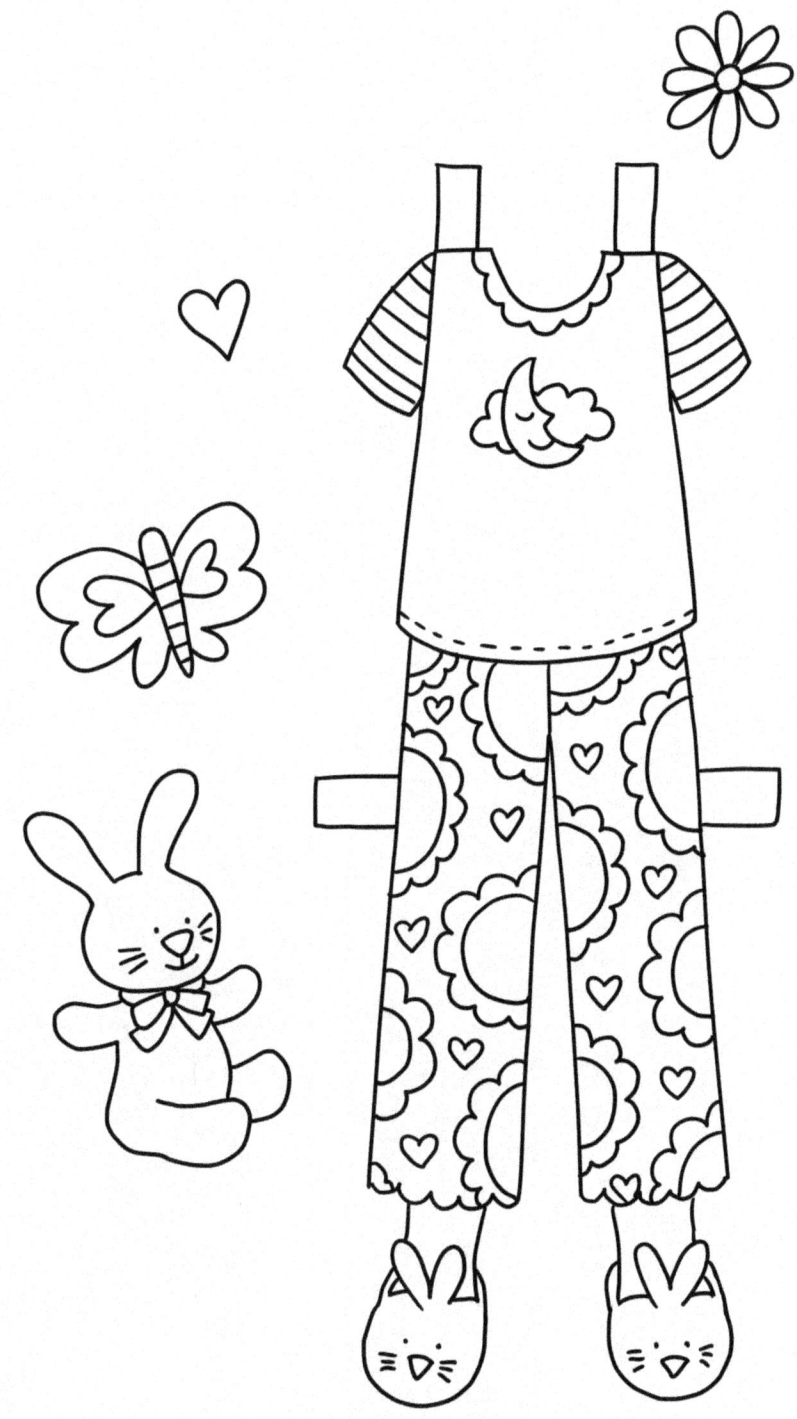

The Coloring Cafe Cuties-Everyday Fun!

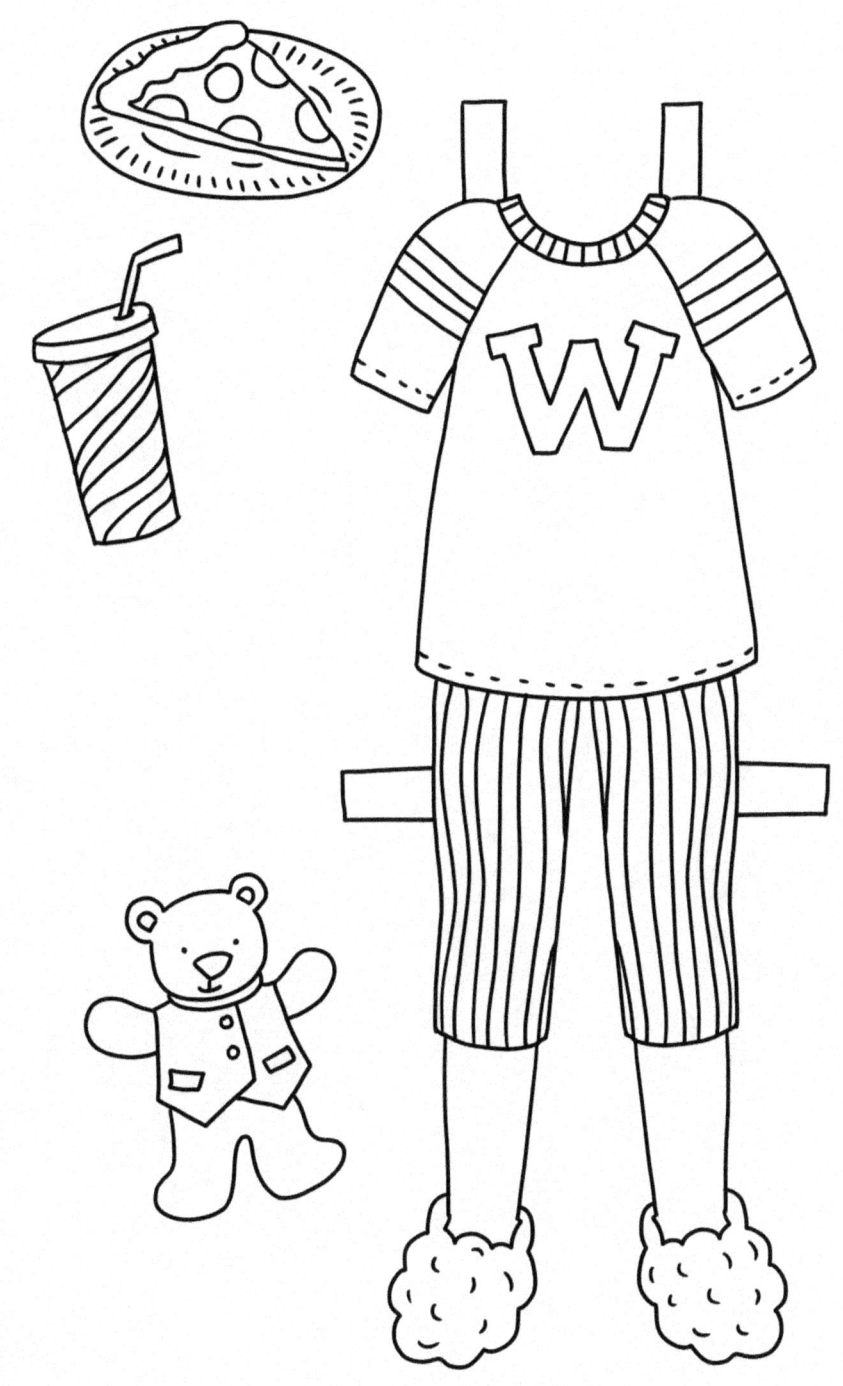

The Coloring Cafe Cuties-Everyday Fun!

About the Artist

Ronnie Walter is an illustrator, writer and art business coach. Her designs can be found on giftware, stationery and greeting cards, home goods and much more. She is also the creator and illustrator behind the popular Coloring Café line of coloring books.

She lives in a little house by the water with her husband Jim Marcotte and their delightful Cathoula rescue dog, Larry.

To contact Ronnie or for more information:
www.ronniewalter.com
www.thecoloringcafe.com